On Life's Unspoken Questions & Concerns

Ultimate Matters Of Personal Meaning

By
Psychologist

"Dr. Dan" Matzke, PhD

For information about other books and programs by
Dr. Dan visit: *DrDanMatzkePhD.com*

About "Dr. Dan"

Dan Matzke, a.k.a. "Dr. Dan", holds a Ph.D. in psychology. Dr. Dan worked as a licensed Psychologist and Marriage & Family Therapist for over 25 years. He taught psychology classes and did consulting work (testing & evaluations), prior to retiring from private practice in California and moving to Jackson Hole, Wyoming. He now enjoys writing and teaching, when not hiking, fishing, skiing, traveling or flying. Dr. Dan has a commercial pilot's license, with flight instructor ratings for airplanes and gliders. He is a winner of the highly prized Barron Hilton Soaring Cup.

Acknowledgements:

Insights and ideas for this program were drawn from many contemporary writers, who have in turn drawn from seminal thinkers and authors throughout history. Interested readers are referred to the books of Irvin D. Yalom, Robert C. Solomon, Carl Rogers, Rollo May, Abraham Maslow and Viktor Frankl.

Disclaimer:

The information provided in this program is informative and educational in nature and is NOT intended as counseling, therapy, psychological treatment and/or psychiatric advice. If you are experiencing acute or chronic emotional problems or symptoms such as anxiety, depression, mood swings, suicidal thoughts, and/or severe symptoms such as auditory hallucinations (hearing voices) or visual hallucinations (seeing things that other people do not see), and/or are feeling overly suspicious or paranoid, and/or are having problems related to drugs or alcohol – it is strongly recommended that you contact a local counseling service, mental health center, psychiatric office and/or your personal medical doctor. Help and hope are available through these sources and you are encouraged to seek it as soon as possible!!

Unspoken Questions & Concerns Addressed in this Program:

Why do I feel so
alone and apart from things at times?

How can I cope with
loneliness and separation in life?

Why is it so difficult to make
choices & commitments?

How can I effectively deal with
freedom & responsibility?

Why do I feel so uncomfortable
with changes?

How can I more effectively cope with
endings in life?

Why do I feel like life is meaningless
and without purpose at times?

How can I find meaning & purpose
in my life?

Why do I feel so much
anxiety & tension at times?

How can I more effectively
deal with stress in life?

Table Of Contents

On Life's Unspoken Questions & Concerns

Preface/Introduction:

This program explores life's unspoken questions and concerns – matters which individuals seldom express to friends or family, and which are not commonly addressed in contemporary psychology, philosophy or religion. These are fundamental questions and concerns which humans have wrestled with throughout all of recorded history, related to Aloneness & Separateness, Choices & Commitments, Meaning & Purpose, and Changes & Endings. Facing and coming to terms with these issues has very liberating and empowering benefits, greatly increasing one's ability to function effectively in personal and professional endeavors. Dealing with these concerns can be rather disquieting. Ultimately, however, recognizing and resolving these matters can free a person to thrive, prosper and succeed.

The core issues considered in this program often overlap and interact with each other, much like the strands of a rope. These are conflicts and dilemmas which all human beings struggle with:

Part 1 - On Aloneness & Separateness:

One of life's primary concerns deals with the personal experience of aloneness and separateness, the sense of being a part of - yet apart from - others and the world around us. We enter into life alone, and we depart, or die alone. Anxiety, tension and conflict results from our awareness of our absolute aloneness, and we wish for contact, protection, and to be a part of a larger whole. No matter how close each of us becomes to another person, there remains a final unbridgeable gap, a separateness between us.

There are three forms of separateness and aloneness which are commonly experienced. One is interpersonal aloneness, a sense of loneliness or social separateness. This has been aggravated by the decline of several social aspects of our culture and lifestyle.

One is the decrease in family involvement. Oftentimes extended family members are several thousand miles apart, spread out and very separate. Church involvement has also gradually declined over the past few generations, reducing social contact. Neighborhoods have become more and more isolated. There is less of a neighborhood feeling and social interaction. These increases in interpersonal isolation over the past several generations have heightened the sense of personal aloneness.

A second type of isolation is intrapersonal - separations within. This often results from splits between our body, mind, and emotions. An example might be a split in which we do not trust our intuition or judgment - there is a split within ourselves. It can involve being out of touch with, or unaware of, one's own body. The mind may be moving alone at warp speed and not be aware of, honoring, or respecting some of the physical needs for nutrition or rest. Other splits might occur because of accepting as absolute, some of the "shoulds" and "oughts" that we were programmed with early in life, over one's own feelings, intuition, or preferences.

A third form of isolation can be referred to as worldly estrangement. This refers to a sense of a separation between one's self and the world, a feeling that you are not part of it all, that you do not fit. A phrase that captures it is that you are "in this world, but not of this world". There is a sense of strangeness. The film "E.T." captured this sense of not being at home, of being alien to the world.

To temper this sense of aloneness and separateness, we can use the world as a tool and absorb ourselves in the means available. Constructive ways through which we can deal with this sense of isolation can be found. One way of dealing with this condition is through creative activity. Creative activity results in a union of the artist with the material or product, a way of bridging the separateness. Another form of creative activity is sport, where a participant experiences a sense of union with the activity or apparatus. A gymnast, for example, can experience flowing movements that often result in a sense of oneness and harmony. The classic example of a Zen archer who is one with his bow and arrow, describes a means of dealing with the sense of separateness.

Another way in which we can deal with aloneness is through group membership, by joining social and professional groups, and by participating in their activities, customs and ceremonies. Participating in group activities helps to deal with feelings of aloneness and separateness. Through becoming part of a larger group or a larger system, we can temper isolation.

A third way of dealing with this basic given is through altered states of consciousness or awareness. Forms of altered states include meditation and prayer, through which a person can experience a sense of unity and oneness. Vigorous rhythmic exercise, such as running, bicycling and swimming, can also result in altered states of consciousness, in which the athlete experiences a sense of balance and harmony.

Perhaps one of the most satisfying ways of dealing with aloneness and separateness is through interpersonal union, or love, where two individuals become one in a relationship, experiencing a sense of closeness and intimacy. Sexual intimacy can result in a profound union including physical, mental and emotional elements. Relationships cannot eliminate isolation, yet aloneness can be shared. Love compensates for the pain of separateness. Relationships can provide a bridge from one alone self to another alone self.

There is however, a dilemma that we encounter in relationships, the dilemma of fusion versus isolation. Fusion... to leech or cling to - versus isolation... to be apart from and alone. This is a major developmental task for human beings; to relate to another person without reducing the other person to a tool, a defense against isolation and its resulting anxiety.

We need to accept the basic human condition of aloneness and separateness, and that it cannot be totally overcome. If not, we may seek desperately to avoid it, or to deny it. This can result in self-defeating and destructive behaviors. One form of self-defeating behavior that is a desperate attempt to overcome isolation is through developing dependent or manipulative relationships. This type of relationship, in which a person is desperately clinging to someone, clutching to them, trying to overcome the sense of aloneness, usually tends to alienate other people, driving them away, which in turn aggravates the aloneness and separateness the person felt originally.

Another extreme form of behavior which attempts to overcome separateness and isolation is fanatical immersion in causes and pursuits. This may include charity work, political causes or religious pursuits. Fanatical emersion often entails constant activity or excessive busyness. Workaholics who have a compulsive drivenness often reflect a desperate attempt to overcome a feeling of being separate, apart or alone.

Another destructive way of trying to avoid this given is through the use of drugs and alcohol, to obtain chemically induced sensations of oneness or harmony. A similar example of attempted escape can be through mysticism. Mysticism involves a sense of ego-loss through experiences of unity or cosmic oneness. This may result in a person "dropping out" of the world, shunning earthly obligations and responsibilities, and going on a relentless quest for mystical experiences in an attempt to overcome the feelings of aloneness and separateness.

Through facing and accepting aloneness and separateness as a given of human existence, we in effect reduce our anxiety and tension, and thereby are less likely to engage in self-defeating actions, in a desperate attempt to avoid or overcome this basic life condition.

Part 2 - On Choices & Commitments:

A second fundamental life concern involves freedom and responsibility. Freedom refers to the absence of external structure, a lack of restrictions and limitations. Human beings have the literal freedom to author their own life design, their choices and commitments. This freedom results in anxiety from the realization that with freedom comes responsibility. If I have the freedom to choose what I shall do, then I am accountable for whatever I choose to do, or choose not to do. To deal with this awesome, anxiety-provoking condition, humans tend to seek structure, to seek out guidelines and rules of authority, as a way of shielding ourselves from absolute freedom. This is done in an attempt to avoid the reality that there are no universal imperatives in life; no absolute shoulds, oughts or musts.

Freedom presents us with the problem of choice. Since there is nothing that we have to do, and there are no absolute universal shoulds or oughts, the question then is "What do you want to do?"

Generally people are not ready for all this freedom. It results in a great deal of anxiety from the realization that one is truly accountable, and ultimately responsible for, one's own life. To avoid this reality a person may engage in a frantic search for someone or something to tell them what to do; to sacrifice one's freedom to avoid the anxiety of being responsible for one's own life. A person may choose to surrender their freedom to an institution, such as a legal or mental health institution, or a belief system, such as a religious dogma, or to another person through a dependent relationship. A person may seek to surrender their freedom, to avoid the responsibility of making choices and commitments.

Another way of shunning self-responsibility is to assume an "ultimate rescuer". This ultimate rescuer is generally viewed as a power that is outside of oneself, that adopts responsibility for us. This notion is often employed to quell anxiety, with the hope for some form of intervention to tell us how to live, or what choices to make. These forms of responsibility avoidance tend to impair a person's effectiveness, and to block mature functioning, which require the acceptance of self-responsibility.

Understanding freedom helps us to deal with responsibility assumption, which involves decision making, choices and commitments. A decision is a very lonely act. Decisions force us to accept personal responsibility, and confront us with anxiety through the realization that we are alone in the choice. It is our choice. A decision, and the resulting commitment, carries with it the connotation of finality. This is it… the impossibility of further possibility. That is the essence of what a decision involves - making a commitment that results in the impossibility of further possibility - the harsh reality that "alternatives exclude".

Many times in life we are faced with an A or B type choice, which can be very anxiety provoking. For then, we are committed to live with our choice, either A or B. As we travel down the road of life we encounter many "forks" in the road. We are repeatedly confronted with the alternatives of either taking the left or right path, with the resulting consequence of never knowing what "might have been" down the other road or choice. Alternatives do exclude. These basic conditions of life, the dilemma of freedom and responsibility, the reality that alternatives often exclude in choices and commitments, cannot be avoided or totally overcome. Through the acceptance of these givens, we can experience a liberating effect from the anxiety inherent in this human predicament, thereby reducing our use of defenses and self-limiting behaviors to deny or avoid these conflicts and dilemmas.

Part 3 - On Changes & Endings:

A third basic life concern deals with changes and endings... the reality that everything fades. The experience of changes and endings in life is often very distressing. The myth of contemporary man is that he is finally in control, that through technology, nature itself can be tamed and made a servant of humanity. Changes and endings confront this myth, and teach us that the universe is vaster than our ability to control it, and more complex than our ability to totally explain it. Few people face or confront changes and endings freely or by choice. Usually life experiences confront us, and these may include changes and endings in relationships, jobs and careers, the loss of a loved one, or near death experiences through accidents or illnesses. If a person is willing to face changes and endings, including his own mortality, instead of avoiding or denying them, many valuable lessons can be learned. A confrontation with a change or ending often results in major shifts in attitudes and behaviors, and a person can make quantum leaps in their personal growth and development.

One of these areas of growth often involves a person's life perspectives and views. There is a realignment of life priorities, of what really matters, of what is important, and what is meaningful. Through facing changes and endings we learn that our unfinished business need not wait until we only have a few weeks, days, or hours to live. Life takes on a new sense of urgency. We do not have time to waste. We cannot really count on tomorrow. Through facing one's finiteness, a person can experience a sense of liberation from some of life's shoulds and oughts. Many of the social customs and rituals are not near as binding, or as restrictive as they once were. The incorporation of our transitoriness enriches life. It enables a person to extricate themselves from many of the smothering trivialities, to live more purposefully, more authentically, to be more open, honest, direct, and to assume more self-responsibility.

Through confronting changes and endings, many people experience an enhanced sense of living in the present... here and now... the idea that each moment can be counted as a gift, one day at a time, one moment at a time. There is much less dwelling on the past or wishful thinking for the future.

Another lesson that many people learn is that they have an increased appreciation and delight in some of the subtle beauties of life, including art, nature and people. Their senses seem to perk up. They tune into some of the subtlest little things. By being mindful of endings, one passes into a state of gratitude, of appreciation for the countless joys of existence.

Many people also experience deeper communication with loved ones, as a result of facing changes and endings. They start talking about things that matter, personal joys and concerns, hopes and dreams. There is a greater willingness to show caring and affection, more hugs, less small talk, less social chitchat and game playing. People start relating person-to-person, stepping out of their roles.

A somewhat paradoxical result of confronting this given is that many people find that they have fewer fears in life. There is a greater willingness to take risks, a desire to live a full life, measured not by the clock and quantity, but by quality, the quality of one's existence. People are not so much afraid of their death as they are afraid of the incompleteness of their life. A person who risks nothing does nothing, has nothing, and is nothing. He may avoid suffering, pain, may postpone death, but he limits his capacity to learn, to grow, and to live. By facing this life given, we find that we have fewer fears, and a greater willingness to take some of the risks that results in a fuller life.

Abraham Maslow, a leader in the field of psychology and education, wrote a letter to a friend after he had a major heart attack. In the letter he said, "The confrontation with death, and the reprieve from it, makes everything look so precious, so sacred, so beautiful, that I feel more strongly than ever the impulse to love it, to embrace it, and to let myself be overwhelmed by it. Death, and its ever-present possibility, makes love, passionate love, more possible. I wonder if we could love, if ecstasy would be possible at all, if we knew we would never die."

Through facing this basic given, each of us feels less futile, less helpless, and less alone, even when ironically what we come to understand is the fact that each of us is basically alone and helpless in the face of universal indifference. Uncertainty exists in life. There are no guarantees. Each of us needs to learn to co-exist with this uncertainty, to tolerate ambiguity, instead of frantically attempting to avoid or control these conditions. Dealing with changes and endings is a letting-go process. It is a skill that is needed and used throughout life. Through acceptance of change and ending as a part of life, including all the small mini-deaths that occur, there is a sense of peace and serenity. The saying "Everything Fades" summarizes it well. Being mindful of this given and surrendering to it gracefully can greatly enhance the joy and satisfaction one experiences in life. Acceptance helps to overcome the notion that changes and endings should be avoided, ought to be fair and just, or must be controlled.

Part 4 - On Life Meaning & Purpose:

A fourth crucial life concern relates to life meaning and purpose. We as human beings tend to be creatures in search for meaning and purpose, and our happiness and well-being is dependent on the extent to which we are able to experience a sense of meaning and purpose in life. Modern man's dilemma is that we are not told by instincts what we must do, or by waning traditions what we should, and oftentimes we do not know what it is that we want to do. The phenomenon of the "Sunday Neurosis" is a common occurrence, in which having free time makes many people aware of the fact that there is nothing that they want to do. Many people struggle with three day weekends. They can keep busy maybe Friday and Saturday, but come Sunday the question arises "What do I want to do with my free time?" When there is a distinct life vacuum, a lack of meaning, symptoms will rush in to fill it. These symptoms often include obsessive/compulsive behaviors such as alcohol and drug abuse, or excessive work.

The workaholic who says, "Gee, I have an extra day, I think I'll go into the office." It can include a variety of delinquent or illegal behaviors, or daredevilry - the taking of risks just for the rush of it, just to get some excitement. These are desperate attempts to fill the void, to overcome the sense of meaninglessness.

At this point in history many people have a lot of free time. Some work four day work weeks. Many have several weeks of vacation time, and oftentimes it is too much free time, in which a person is confronted with some disturbing questions. Free time is problematic because it confronts us with the question of what to do with our time. What is meaningful? What is satisfying? What should I do? What do I really want to do with my life? The issue of life meaning and purpose is one that human beings have wrestled with throughout all of recorded history. As human beings we have the capacity to be self-aware, to step outside of our self, to assume a detached view. This capacity for self-awareness and self-detachment can be very valuable and powerful. It also has some risks, however. There is a danger. There are some problems which occur when we step back too far, or when we stay there too long. When we assume a cosmic view or galactic perspective of life, we can get into trouble. This detached viewpoint tends to drain vitality from life. To assume it for a prolonged period of time can result in a sense of despair, and continued emersion in a detached viewpoint may be lethal. It can result in severe depression and suicidal thoughts. There is a saying that sums it up quite well: "Analysis leads to paralysis". If we are very busy analyzing life, asking all sorts of "why" or "what for" questions, we tend to get paralyzed. We are impaired. Our ability to engage in life, to fully participate, is blocked. The direct quest for the ultimate meaning of life can be a self-sabotaging endeavor.

The search for life meaning is paradoxical in that the more we search for it, the less we find it. A frantic search for the "goal" or "point" of life can lead to a sense of meaninglessness and despair - that nothing matters from a cosmic view or galactic perspective.

The answer, a sense of meaning and purpose in life, is found by looking away from the question, by disengaging from the cosmic viewpoint, and by engaging in life. Life is a gift. Take it, unwrap it, appreciate it, use it and enjoy it. Regardless of one's religious beliefs, philosophical views, or scientific approach to life, all humans are confronted with the same basic challenge of finding meaning and purpose in life. Although half-sure, we can wholeheartedly leap into engagement, immersing oneself in the stream of life... being fully present, here and now... getting into being human and the process of being.

There are three primary means to personal meaning and purpose. One is through creativity. Creativity in what we do, what we give to the world, in how we use our time and energy. This could include work, hobbies, sports, and service to others. Some examples might include art and teaching, caring relationships, or scientific discovery. To create or discover something new, to put something together in a different way, something of beauty, something of harmony. As for the question of "Why?" or "What for?" – For its own sake. It really needs no excuse or reason. Creativity is intrinsically rewarding and satisfying in and of itself. The creative process of using our time and energy results in joy and well-being. It is personally meaningful.

A second means to meaning is through experiences that we have - what we take in and what we get from the world. Through experiencing truth, beauty, the love of another human being, we experience a sense of meaning and purpose in life. Tuning into the natural order around us, tuning into the subtle and delicate balances in life, tuning into the harmony which exists, being aware of it, appreciating it, and delighting in it, results in a meaningful existence.

A third means to meaning centers on our attitude – our thinking and focus in life. Negative thinking tends to focus on "what is not" or "what cannot be", and results in a great deal of frustration and disappointment. In contrast, by focusing on "what is" and "what can be", life meaning and purpose looms. Meaning potentials and opportunities take form, and give us direction and purpose in life.

By not getting caught up in the thinking that one should or must have an answer to the question of "What's the ultimate meaning of life?", a person is freer to experience a sense of personal meaning and purpose in life, through passionate engagement, by doing and experiencing what is, and what can be.

Part 5 - On Anxiety, Tension & Stress:

A fifth pervasive life concern is the stressful feeling of anxiety and tension, the sense of uncertainty, apprehension, uneasiness and pressure, which is a part of the human condition. It is an illusion to think that this condition can ever be completely overcome or avoided. With the human capacity for consciousness and awareness, comes the ability to see possibilities, many of which can be very distressing. These possibilities include not only the opportunity for success, joy, health, and happiness, but also the possibility or chance of failure, sadness, illness, and despair. This uniquely human capacity is a double edged sword, which requires a delicate balance to be used effectively. Each individual has a "comfort zone" of anxiety and tension, within which they can function. Too much or too little tension results in discomfort and impairment. It is a basic challenge in life to maintain this baseline of anxiety and tension within one's personally acceptable limits. For example with work, it is a challenge to maintain a level of demand and pace which is a balance between being bored and being overwhelmed. In physical and emotional endeavors, it is a challenge to maintain the delicate balance of "total control" versus "total chaos" or safety and security versus taking risks. It is a continual challenge to maintain the delicate balance between being totally engaged, and being detached, in the three arenas of life: love, work, and play.

Through engagement, we become immersed in the process of doing and experiencing life. Active involvement results in "losing oneself", including one's troubles and concerns. While this effectively reduces anxiety and tension, total, continual engagement results in the risk of getting lost, of being consumed, or going off on a tangent, which can be self-defeating and destructive.

Through detachment, a person can extricate themselves from the activities and busyness of life, and objectively observe the process with dispassionate regard. This perspective can result in a clear view of life's complexities, allowing an individual to guide and direct the course of their life. However, continued detachment results in an escalation of anxiety and tension, leading to a sense of apathy or despair, a feeling that nothing matters, or that it's all futile.

By balancing engagement and detachment, anxiety and tension can be maintained at an acceptable level. Through finding a personal balance in love, work and play, and striving to maintain this level within one's comfort zone, a person is better able to deal with anxiety and tension, which is a stressful life given.

In Summary

The five fundamental life questions and concerns reviewed often overlap and interact with each other, much like the strands of a rope. These are basic conflicts and dilemmas which all human beings struggle with:

1) No matter how close we get to another person, we still face life alone.

2) Each person has the ultimate responsibility for their choices and commitments, no matter how much guidance and advice they get from others.

3) Change is perhaps the only permanent thing in life, with many life changes and endings being unfair and unjust.

4) We can experience a sense of personal meaning and purpose in life, in spite of not having a definitive answer to the question "What is the ultimate meaning of life?"

5) Anxiety and tension is a normal part of life, which cannot be totally overcome, only kept in balance.

There are no "fixes", so to speak, no way to do away with these anxiety-provoking conditions of life. Through facing and accepting of the reality of how it is, we can experience liberation from the frantic and desperate attempt to avoid or overcome these givens, and from the thinking that things should be, ought to be, or must be, different, for us to be happy. Through acceptance, we can experience a sense of peace and serenity, which frees us to live life more fully and richly, in more effective and successful ways.

<u>Addendum</u>

"Wings Of Wisdom"

Uplifting Essence Essays

By Psychologist

"Dr. Dan" Matzke, PhD

On Life & Living
Seven Golden Guidelines

On Personal Effectiveness
Seven Powerful Pointers

On The Art & Technique Of
Mindfulness

On Life & Living
Seven Golden Guidelines

By Psychologist "Dr. Dan" Matzke, PhD

Truth
Seek truth, truthfulness and genuineness.
Be real, honest and sincere,
And seek others who are authentic.

Beauty
Look for beauty and good in nature, art and people.
Appreciate aesthetic magnificence and grandeur.

Excellence
Strive for excellence and quality in all endeavors.
Enjoy the elements of grace and elegance.

Wisdom
Seek wisdom and the prudent use of knowledge.
Aim to use good reasoning and judgment.

Justice
Strive for justice, fairness and reasonableness.
Be compassionate and caring with integrity.

Courage
Have the courage to stand for that which is best.
Be courageous with valor and gallantry.

Moderation
Seek balance and harmony in life.
Exercise moderation and temperance in living.

Author's Note: The above thoughts, ideas and perspectives are drawn from great seminal thinkers throughout all of recorded history. These are wise time-tested principles which can be powerful tools - useful in guiding one's daily actions toward life success and happiness. Interested readers are referred to classical writings in literature, philosophy and spirituality for further study. Other programs and books by Dr. Dan are available at *DrDanMatzkePhD.com* PS – You are invited to share this essay.

>>>>>>><<<<<<<

On Personal Effectiveness
Seven Powerful Pointers

By Psychologist "Dr. Dan" Matzke, PhD

Planning
Think ahead - be proactive.
Prioritize and organize future actions.

Preparedness
Aim for anticipation and prevention.
Strive to be ready for future needs.

Pacing
Aspire for flow without force.
Adjust the pace to fit the place.

Persistence
Endeavor for progress and progression.
Take the steps one at a time.

Perspective
For best perspective - be objective.
Seek to see the big picture.

Patience
Be here – now.
Question the need to hurry or rush.

Personal-Responsibility
Focus on choices and commitments.
Get real... Get a grip... Get on with it.

Author's Note: While the above pointers are basic and primary, they are critical and essential for personal effectiveness. The guideposts can also point to matters that one is ignoring or avoiding (due to fear, dread, etc.) which are road blocks and barriers towards the next step and/or the next level in one's endeavors and life journey. A good "rule of thumb" is that ten percent (10%) extra effort invested in using these principles results in a ninety percent (90%) difference. Developing one's awareness of and practicing these pointers and self-coaching tools can yield significant benefits – enabling one to "take a hold of life" and face challenges with courage and confidence. Other programs and books by Dr. Dan are available at *DrDanMatzkePhD.com* PS - You are invited to share this essay.

>>>>>>><<<<<<<

On The Art & Technique Of
Mindfulness

Powerful Principles & Practices
For Personal Development,
Peak Performance & Well-Being

By Psychologist "Dr. Dan" Matzke, PhD

This essence essay considers the art and technique of mindfulness – which can be described as a mental state of clear minded awareness that is unencumbered, unfettered and unhurried. The art of mindfulness entails being fully present to experience and savor being alive, awake and aware. The technique of mindfulness involves consciously focusing one's attention on thoughts, feelings and actions, many of which can at times be self-defeating and toxic. Three core issues can be identified which often overlap and interact with each other, much like the strands of a rope. These are natural tendencies and habit patterns which all human beings struggle with:

Keep Critical, Judgmental & Negative Thinking
In Check

Nurture
Positive Perspectives

Temper Unfounded
Fears & Self-Doubts

Develop A
Trusting Attitude

Be Cautious Of Consumption By
The Past & The Future

Practice Being Present
Here & Now

Author's Note: The above principles of mindfulness are time-tested realistic practices, which were first articulated over 2500 years ago. These ideas are powerful pointers and skills which can greatly enhance personal effectiveness and well-being. Other programs and books by Dr. Dan are available at *DrDanMatzkePhD.com* PS - You are invited to share this essay.